EASY PIANO SOLOS

Jazz

ISBN 978-1-61774-208-8

HAL•LEONARD® CORPORATION
7777 W. BLUEMOUND RD. P.O. BOX 13819 MILWAUKEE, WI 53213

Visit Hal Leonard Online at
www.halleonard.com

BEYOND THE SEA

Lyrics by JACK LAWRENCE
Music by CHARLES TRENET
and ALBERT LASRY
Original French Lyric to "La Mer" by
CHARLES TRENET

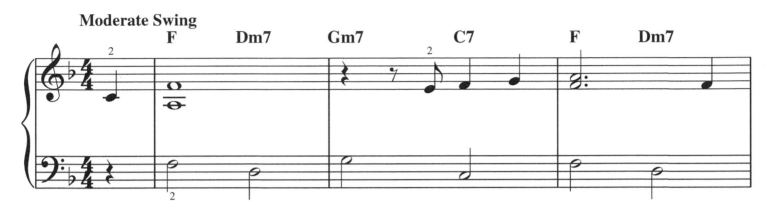

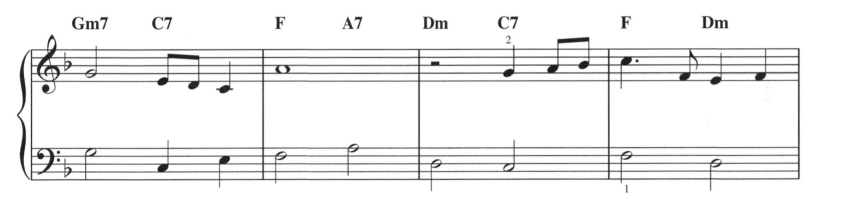

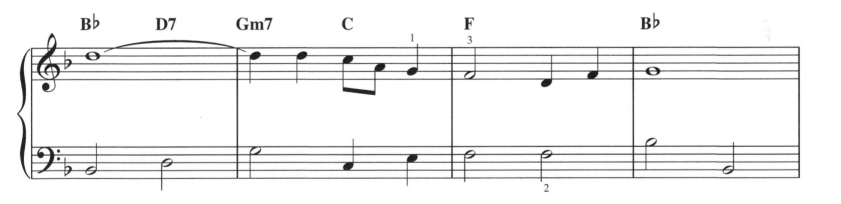

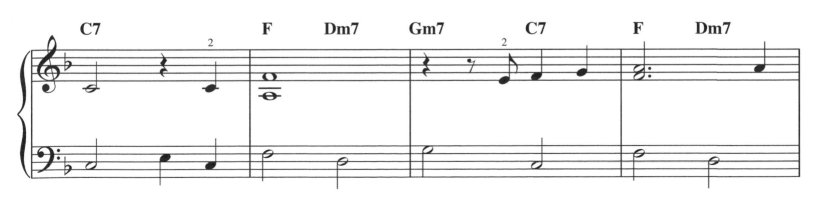

4

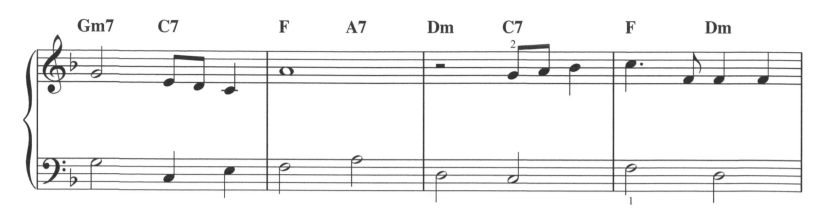

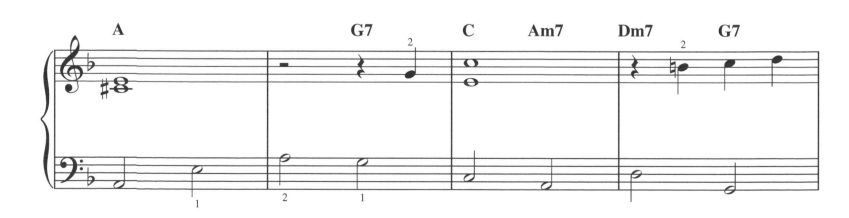

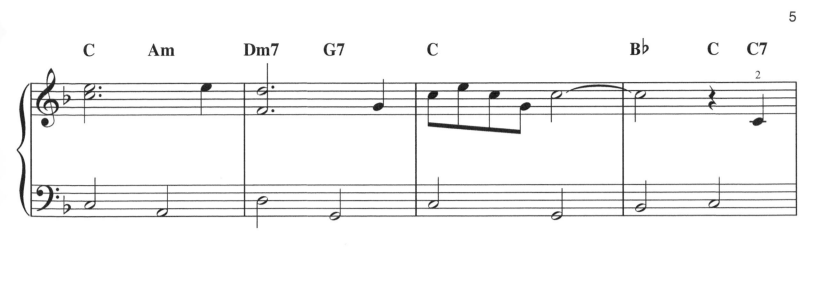

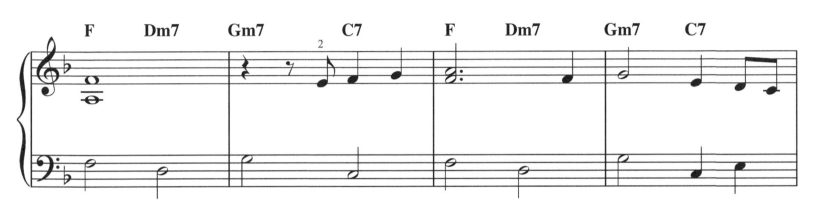

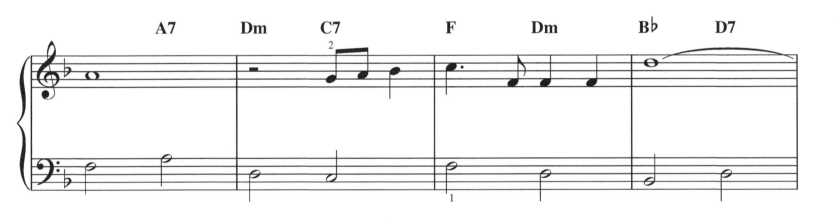

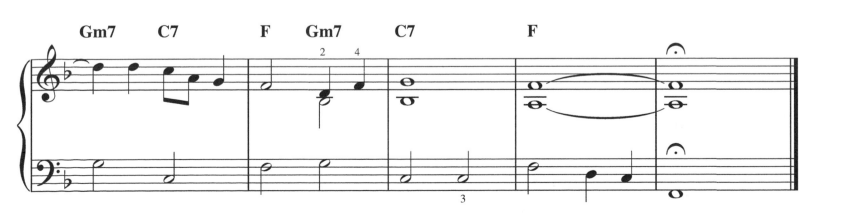

ALL BLUES

By MILES DAVIS

Cool Swing

Always quiet and smooth

ALL THE THINGS YOU ARE

Lyrics by OSCAR HAMMERSTEIN II
Music by JEROME KERN

Moderately, with expression

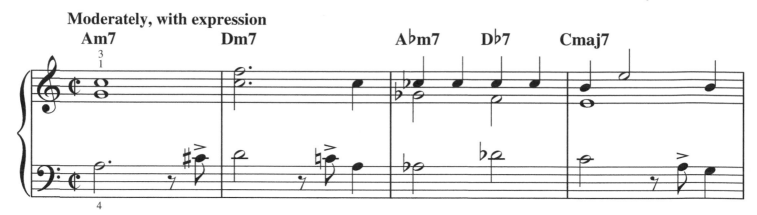

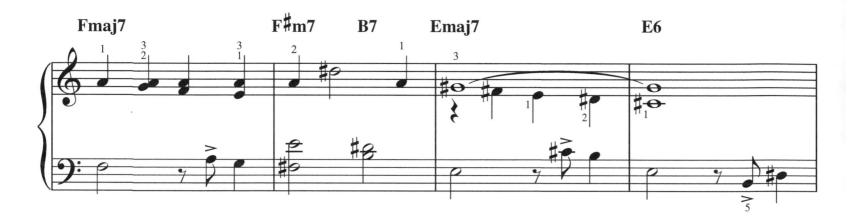

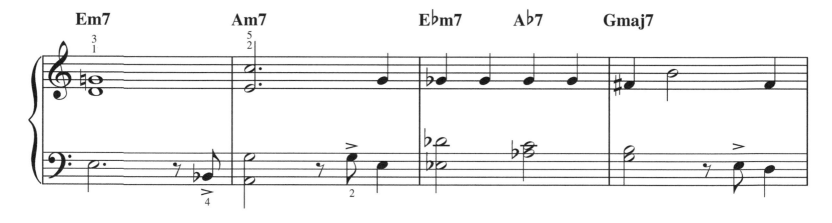

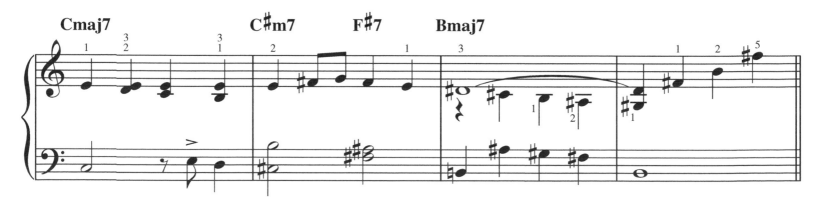

ANGEL EYES

Words by EARL BRENT
Music bt MATT DENNIS

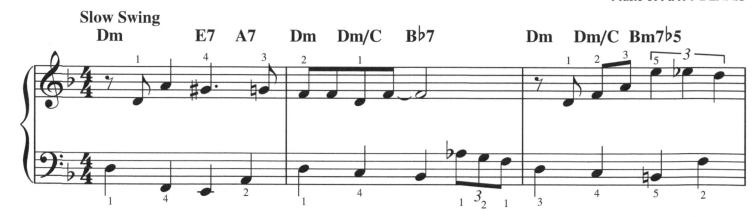

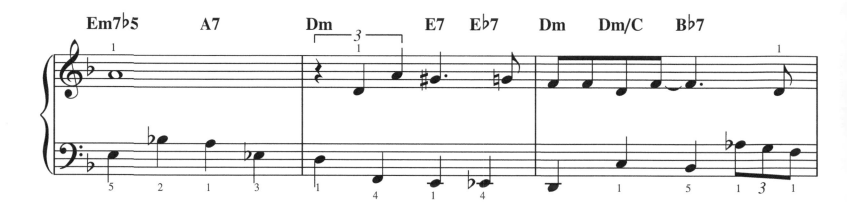

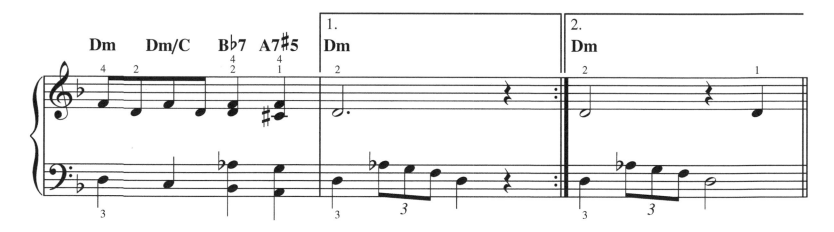

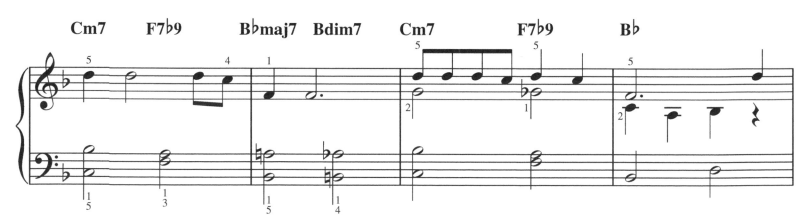

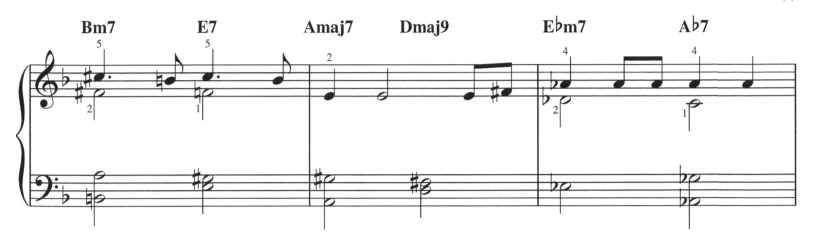

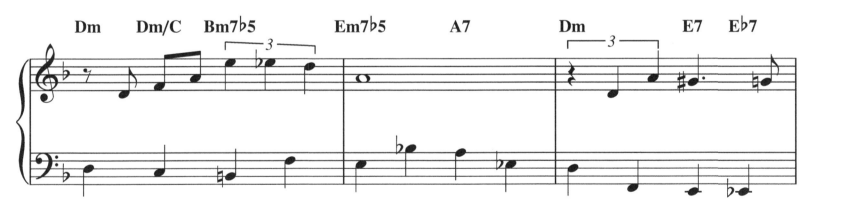

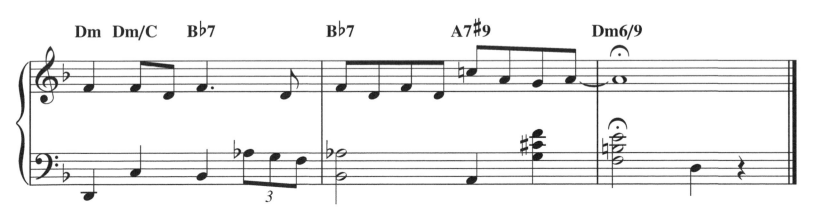

CARAVAN

Words and Music by DUKE ELLINGTON,
IRVING MILLS and JUAN TIZOL

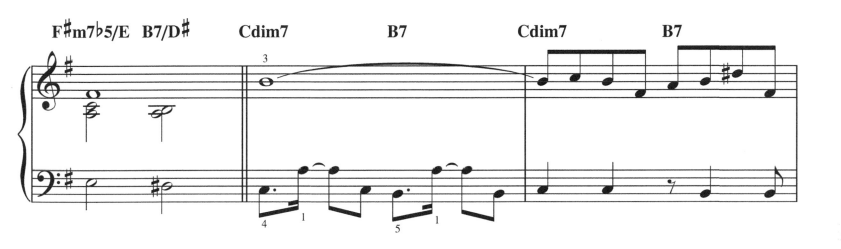

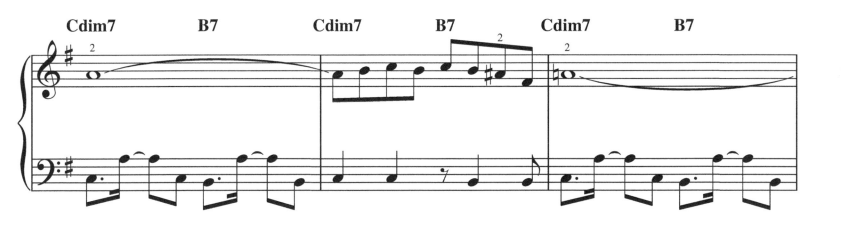

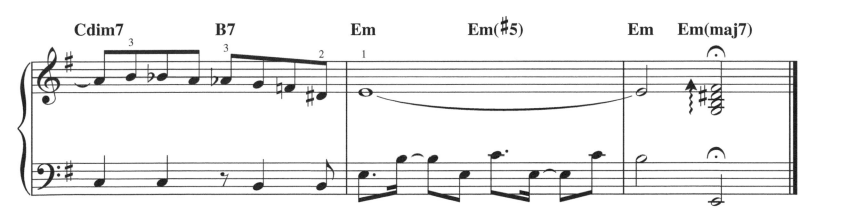

DO NOTHIN' TILL YOU HEAR FROM ME

Words and Music by DUKE ELLINGTON
and BOB RUSSELL

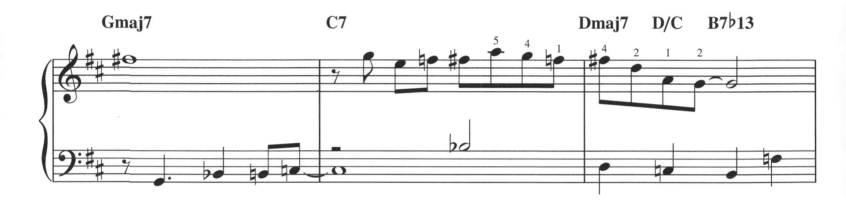

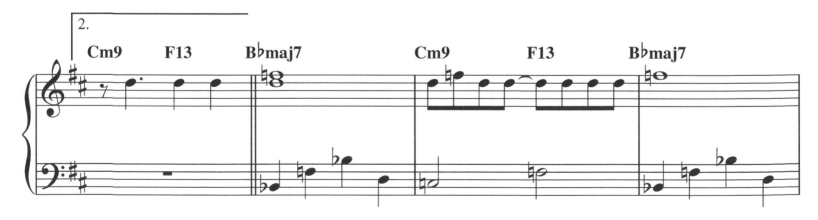

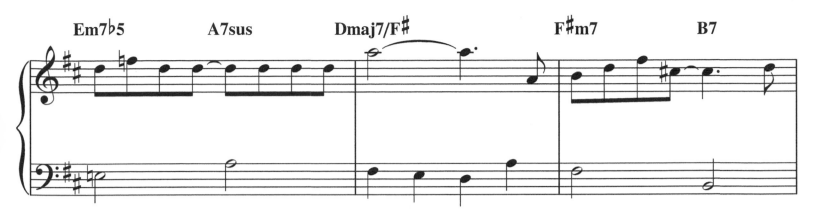

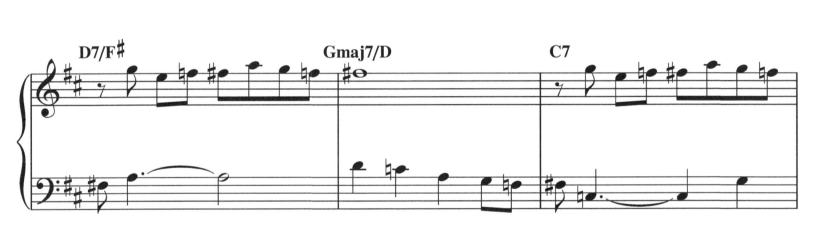

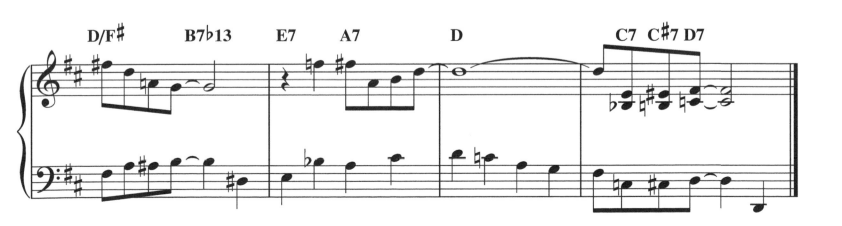

FLY ME TO THE MOON
(In Other Words)

Words and Music by
BART HOWARD

With celestial spirit

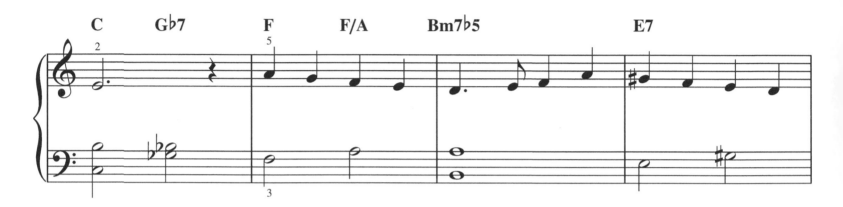

THE GIRL FROM IPANEMA
(Garôta de Ipanema)

Music by ANTONIO CARLOS JOBIM
English Words by NORMAN GIMBEL
Original Words by VINICIUS DE MORAES

19

GIRL TALK

By NEAL HEFTI

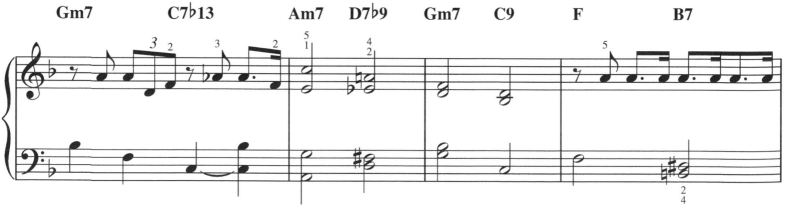

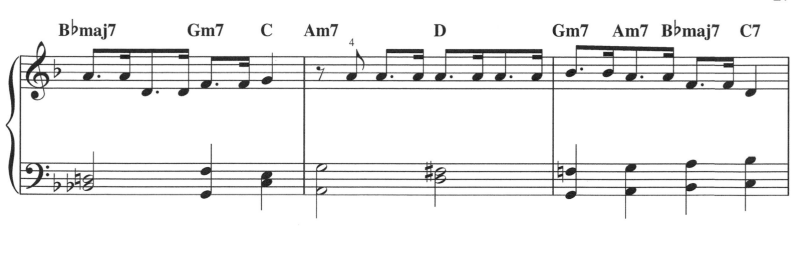

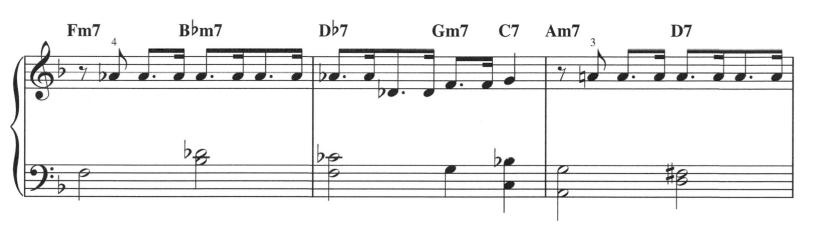

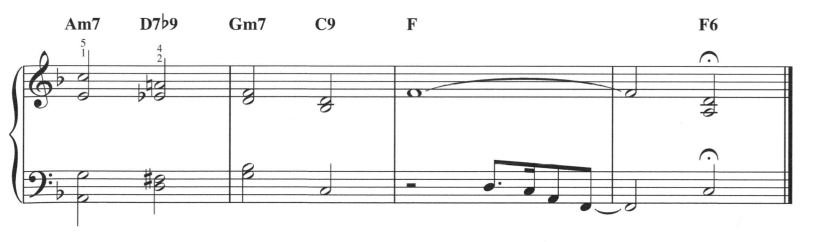

GOD BLESS' THE CHILD

Words and Music by ARTHUR HERZOG JR.
and BILLIE HOLIDAY

HERE'S THAT RAINY DAY

Words by JOHNNY BURKE
Music by JIMMY VAN HEUSEN

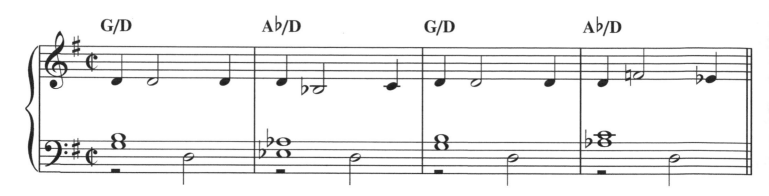

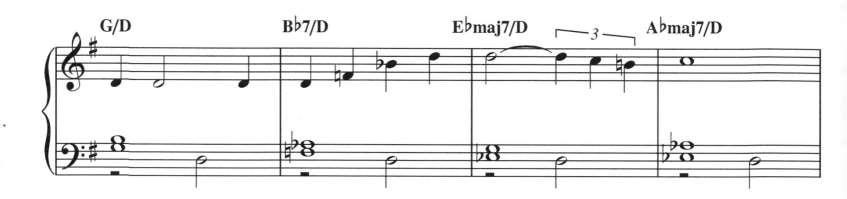

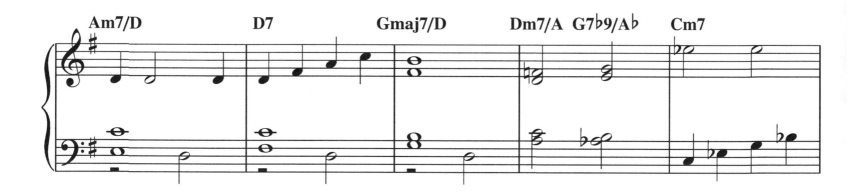

I'M BEGINNING TO SEE THE LIGHT

Words and Music by DON GEORGE,
JOHNNY HODGES, DUKE ELLINGTON
and HARRY JAMES

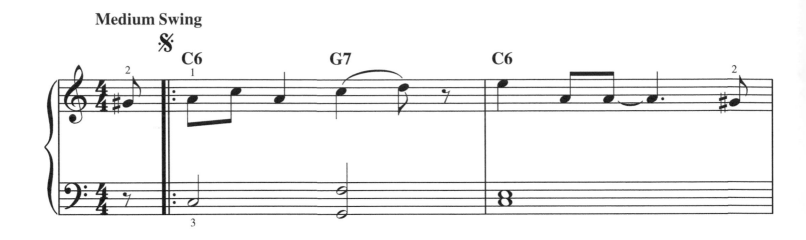

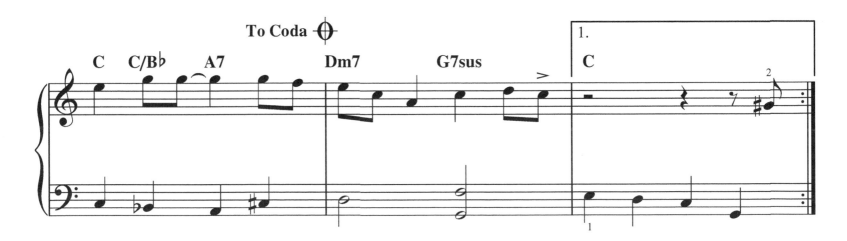

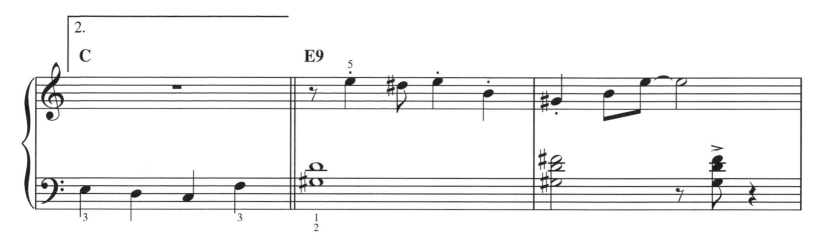

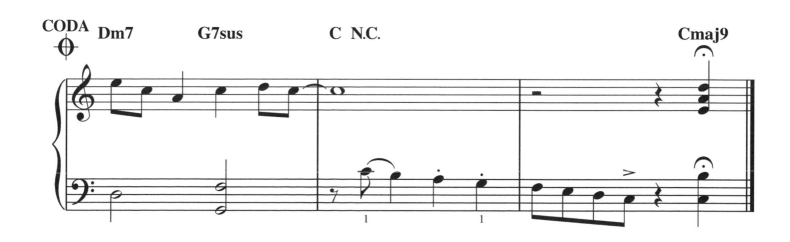

IN WALKED BUD

By THELONIOUS MONK

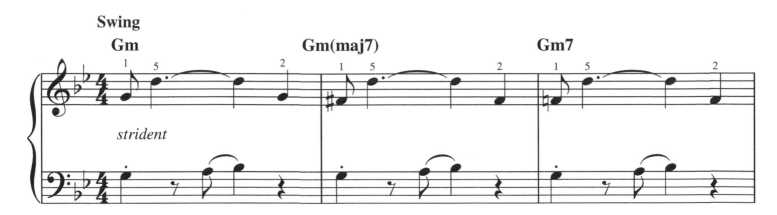

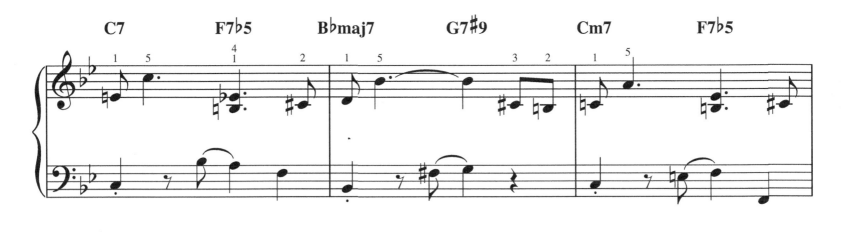

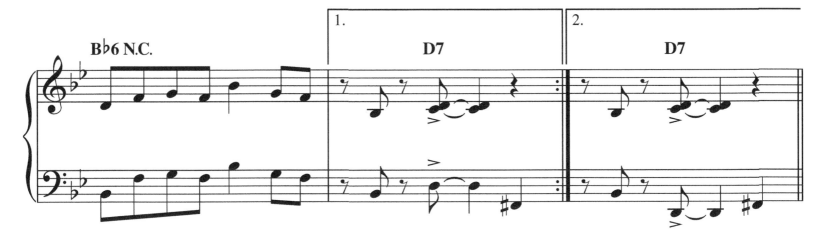

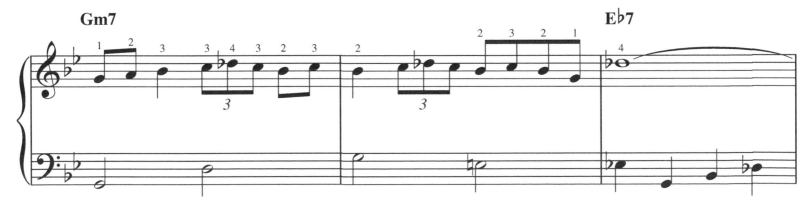

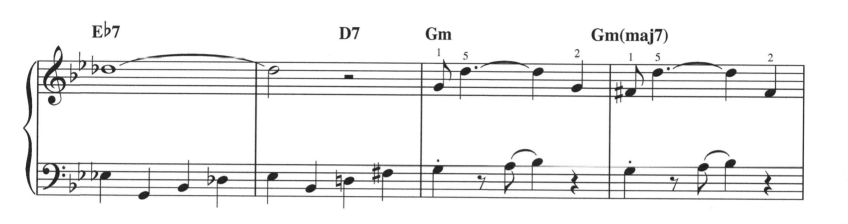

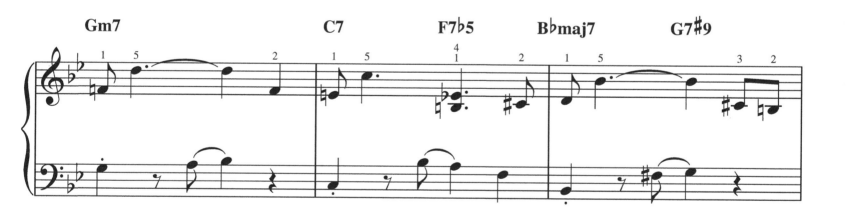

ONE NOTE SAMBA
(Samba de uma nota so)

Original Lyrics by NEWTON MENDONÇA
English Lyrics by ANTONIO CARLOS JOBIM
Music by ANTONIO CARLOS JOBIM

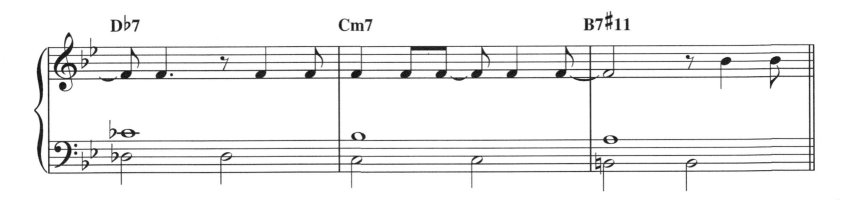

32

WALTZ FOR DEBBY

Lyric by GENE LEES
Music by BILL EVANS

Jazz Waltz, in 1

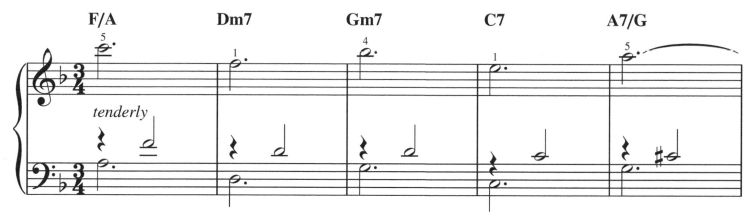

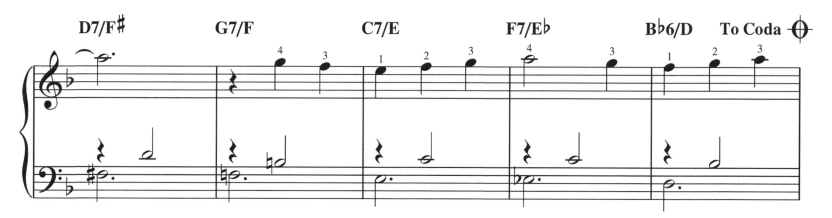

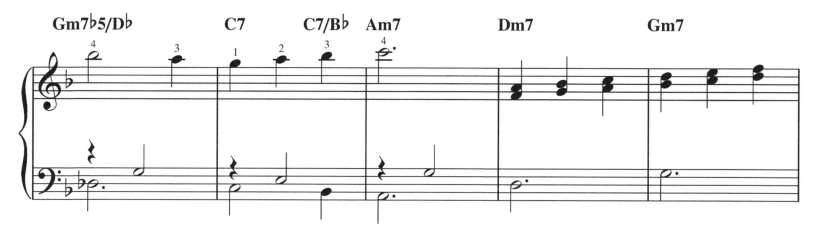

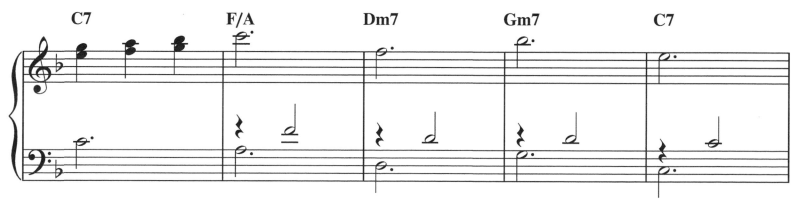

34

SATIN DOLL

By DUKE ELLINGTON

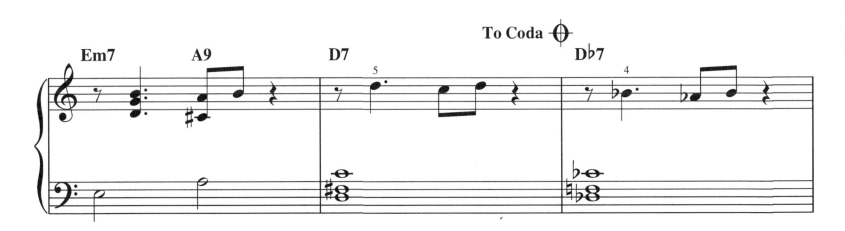

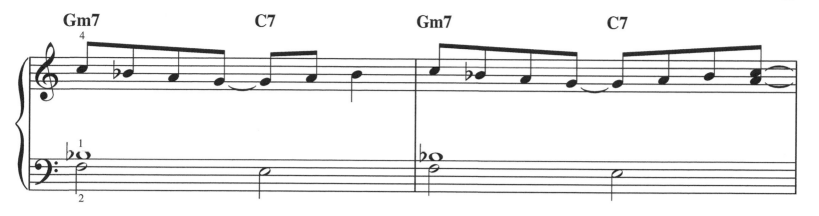

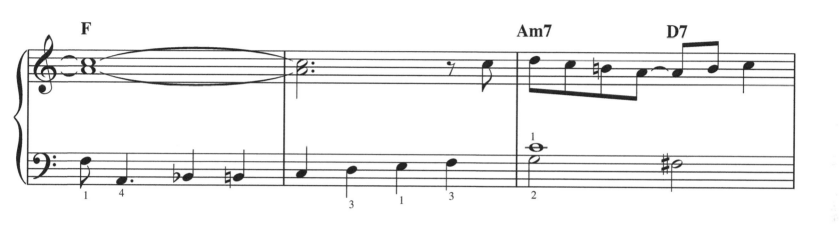

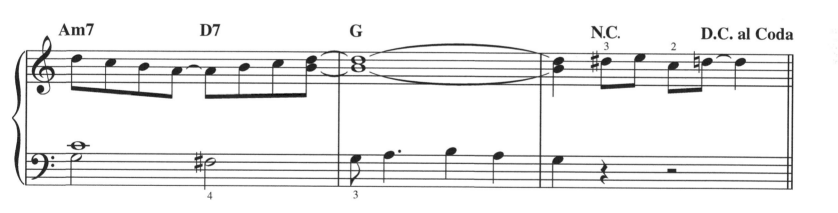

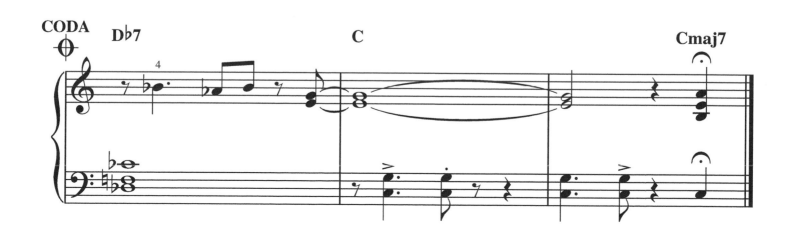

SO WHAT

By MILES DAVIS

TAKE THE "A" TRAIN

Words and Music by
BILLY STRAYHORN

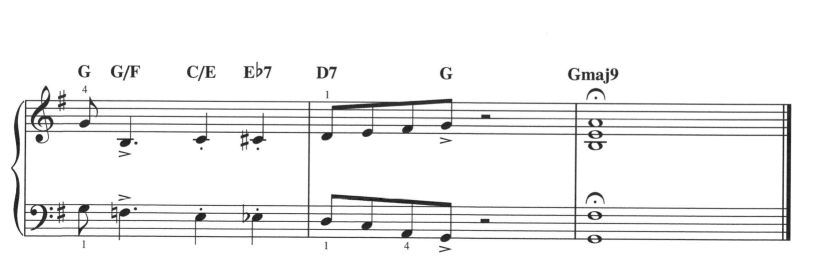

THE VERY THOUGHT OF YOU

Words and Music by
RAY NOBLE

Freely

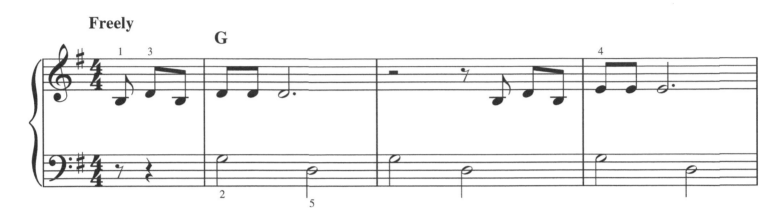

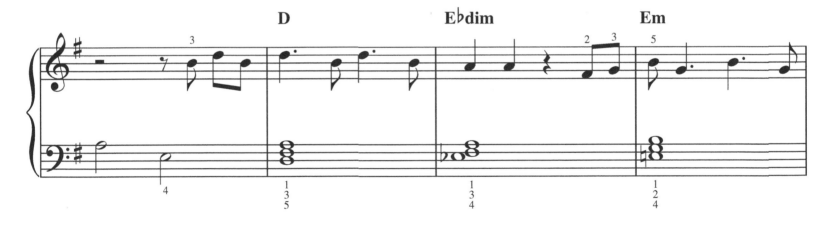

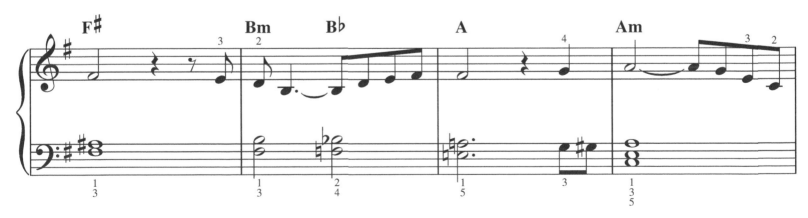

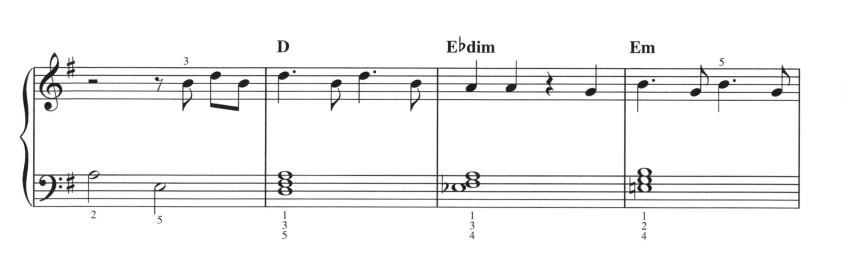

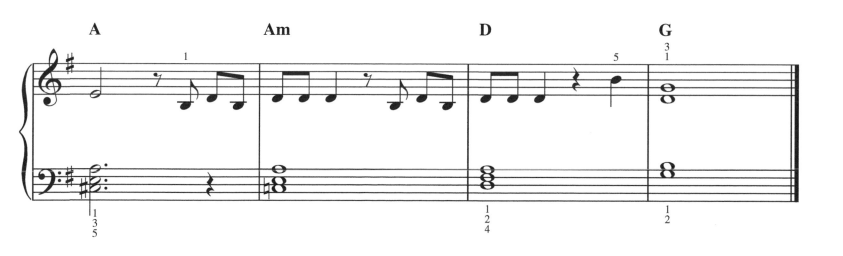

THE WAY YOU LOOK TONIGHT

Words by DOROTHY FIELDS
Music by JEROME KERN

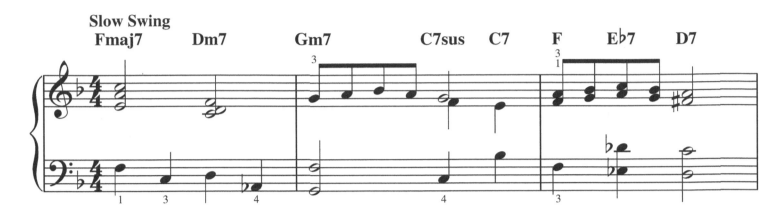

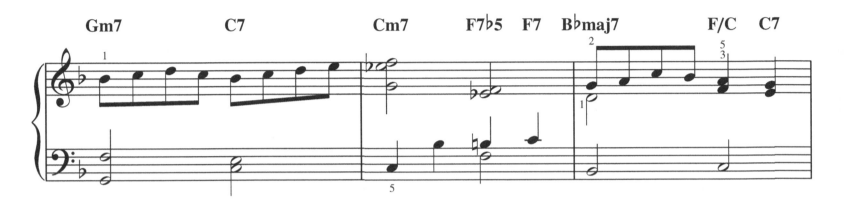

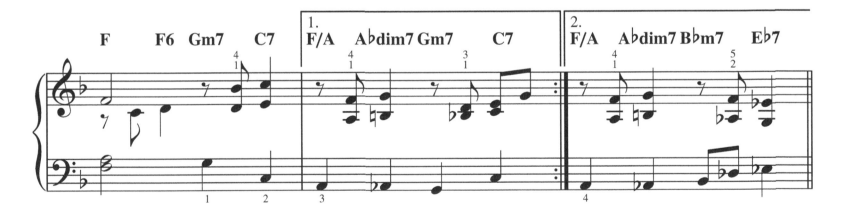

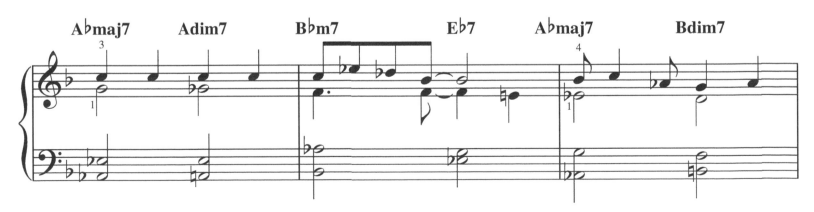

YOU BROUGHT A NEW KIND OF LOVE TO ME

Words and Music by SAMMY FAIN,
IRVING KAHAL and PIERRE NORMAN

Laid-back Swing

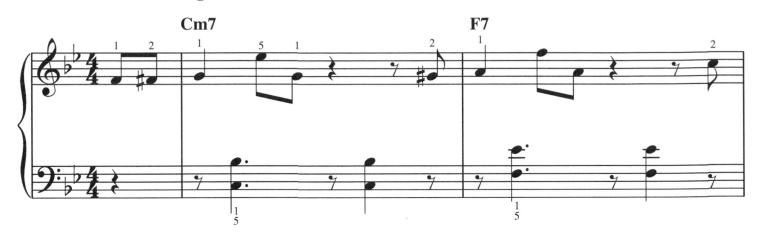

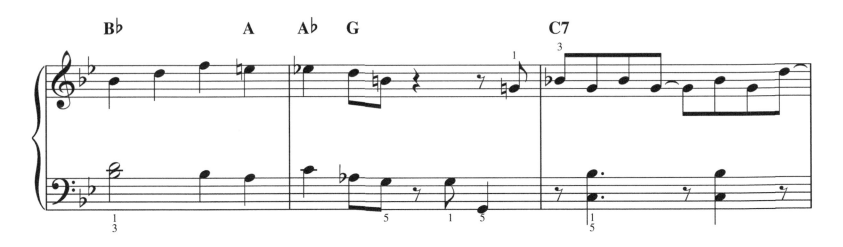

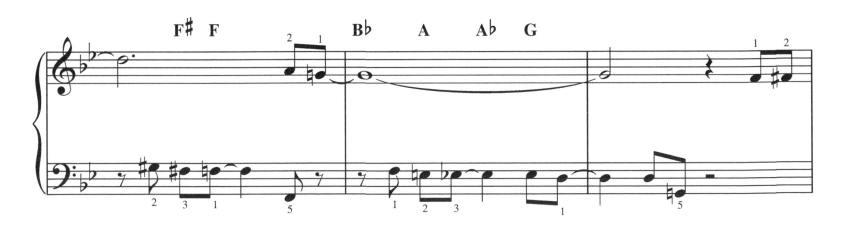

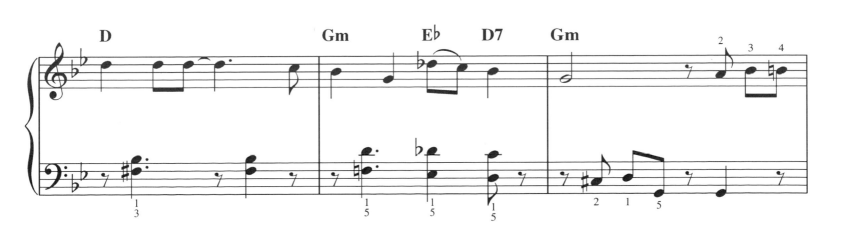

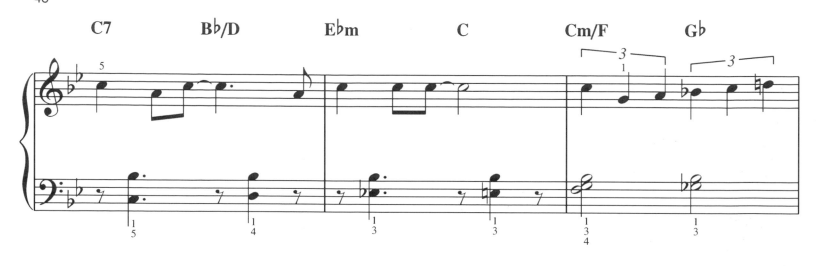

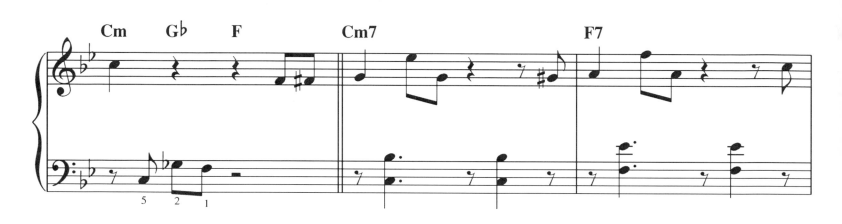